THE BROKEN GUITAR

 A catalogue record for this book is available from the National Library of Australia

© Richard Greene

Published 2021

ISBN: 978-0-6453006-3-5 (ebook)
ISBN: 978-0-6453006-4-2 (paperback)
ISBN: 978-0-6453006-5-9 (pdf)

Published with the aid of Jumble Books and Publishers (jumblebooksandpublishers.com)

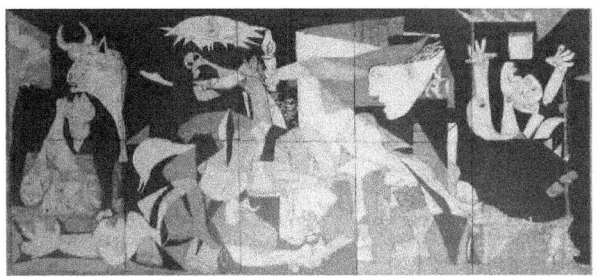

Image credit:
Guernica City Hall Pforzheim (Germany) by
Moleskine, 12 May 2017 (CC BY-SA 4.0)

The Broken Guitar

Poems of War

by

Richard Greene

Richard Greene is a poet, or has been at least since he retired from a 38-year career in international development. A lawyer by training, he fell into his development career by accident when, after law school, though planning not to practice law but interested in international affairs, he accepted an unsolicited job offer from the U.S. Agency for International Development. After a few years in Washington (or Foggy Bottom, as the location of the U.S. foreign policy establishment is known), he was assigned as legal advisor to the USAID mission in Laos and there discovered that the development business suited his interests and inclinations very well.

Greene wrote poetry beginning in the 8th grade and continued through college where he studied with a Professor, Henry Rago, who later became editor of *Poetry* magazine, the leading U.S. poetry journal. However, he wrote few poems after law school as he became absorbed in international development, but turned back to poetry as he neared retirement.

To my wife, Celeste, who helps me in countless ways, including multiple editing inputs.

Contents

Memorial Day 1
Victoriana 3
A Century's Wars 4
A Gentler Time 5
The Charms of War 6
The Broken Guitar 7
Your Grandfather's War 8
When the British Sank the Tirpitz 9
The Last Veteran 10
September 1, 1939.. 11
December 7, 1941 12
A Boy's War 13
In Memory of.. 14
The Veterans... 15
I Was a Soldier Once 16
Citizen Soldier.. 17
Vor der Kaserne 18
Aftermath 19
Roll Call... 20
Remembering Vientiane 21
Lahore 22
Angkor 23
Martyrs: Afghanistan 24
Boots on the Ground 25
Forward to the Past... 26

The Things They Carry 27
Where Have All the Young Men Gone? 28
All the Brave Men 29
Memorial 30
The Unnamed Dead 31
Numbers Don't Speak 32
The Grenade 33
The Weapons Economy 34
The Great and the Good 35
To Those without Whom We Couldn't Win 36

Memorial Day

Hopewell, New Jersey, May 2005

It was enough to make us weep,
half a dozen veterans of the last great war
looking like fading away,
followed by the high school band,
booming bravely into adulthood.
Next a squad in Civil War uniform,
harking back to the source of the holiday,
a fratricide that seems today
to have occurred in another country,
not just another century.
A retired Humvee
with a small girl in back
wearing a grunt-style cap
and waving mechanically;
vintage cars,
big ones from a century ago
with wooden spokes
and other vestiges of their carriage genes,
still boxy ones from the 20s,
the streamlined 30s,
the fishtailed 50s,
a couple of Mustangs, an early Corvette;
then the fire engines, big and bigger,
like armor-plated rhinos,
our town's brigade riding old fashioned red,
others yellow,
sage green from a well-heeled town nearby;
delegations of Boy Scouts, Cub Scouts, Brownies,
one scout troop with a five-piece band
trying like twenty-five;
a motorcycle club,
plenty of paunch and gray hair,

and, though some ponytails,
suburban angels rather than Hells.
Finally, a platoon of kids
all safely helmeted,
one tireless on a pogo stick
others on scooters and bikes
and even a few on tricycles,
training for future wars.

Victoriana

These houses were built before WWII,
the Third Reich,
the Holocaust,
before WWI even,
before Korea, Vietnam, Rwanda, Iraq,
Hitler, Stalin, Mao, Pol Pot.
Walking by these houses
this pleasant spring evening
I imagine those living in them
so many years before,
in the warm glow of gas lamps,
untroubled by awareness
of atrocities or war.

A Century's Wars

I'm not good at birthdates
but have always remembered my stepfather's,
for his was the day the Great War ended.
We have a photo of him in France,
on a hill overlooking the Rhine,
a tall, clean-shaven, young marine
in breeches, boots and campaign hat
hands on hips, legs spread,
seeming to tower like a monument
over the river's far bank.

There's another photo of him,
on Saipan,
carbine in hand,
soiled battle fatigues,
helmet with chin strap hanging open,
looking smaller than I'd ever seen him look.
That was the day his friend's son died there,
a friend he'd carried from a battlefield in France.

A Gentler Time

As I did the dishes tonight
they were playing Debussy on the radio,
the Preludes, from 1913,
and I thought
Oh to have been in Paris then,
the Paris of Rodin, Monet, Picasso, Proust
a gentler, more contemplative time,
on the eve of the Great War.

The Charms of War

It was a good war,
World War I,
for us Americans
who were in it only briefly
and didn't lose so many young men.
It had its compensations,
its mademoiselles,
its Hemingway,
old Europe
with its worldly charms,
and our heroically coming to its rescue.
Then tickertape parades
down lower Broadway,
and the best of times
in left bank cafés.
Would we have been there
if not for the war?

Then World War II
less romantic, true,
but righteous,
a war against evil,
the best of wars.
And even less virtuous wars,
food for nostalgia even there,
for we love war
and will, I suppose,
as long as men grow from boys.

The Broken Guitar

There was a photo in the book review
of First World War dead,
Italians killed by Austrians
the caption said.
Italians? Austrians?
They haven't made war on each other
for nearly a century.
Yet there the Italians lie
in a row
as if asleep in a dormitory
except that their bodies are strangely twisted
and too dirty for sleeping men,
as if mud had flowed over them
trying to bury these mothers' sons,
and on the ground
next to one of them
a muddy guitar
its head broken off.

Your Grandfather's War

Your grandfather fought in "the great war".
He was in a famous battle in France
wounded with shrapnel and mustard gassed,
may have shot at the enemy and been shot at—
I never asked—
may even have fought hand-to-hand
where you can see the grime on your enemy's face
and the fear in his eyes
over the frantic thrust and parry of your bayonet
and his
and feel the frenzy of your own fear.

Now that war is history
so remote you can read of it
innocent of the feelings
of those who faced each other
in an effort to kill
and survive.

When the British Sank the Tirpitz

the colossal vessel capsized
trapping many sailors
against the hull inside
in a rising tide.
Rescue crews raced to locate the men
shouting and knocking within
and cut through the thick hull
with welding torches,
but the tide rose faster
till many of the still trapped men
had no room to breathe,
and their voices fell silent.

Those men were supporters, of course,
of an evil regime,
but were we to have an evil regime
would our fighting men support it any the less?

The Last Veteran

He was our last veteran of our grandfathers' war
the war to end all wars,
five wars ago.
After all the others had gone
he bore the memory alone,
of mud, trenches, blasted trees,
that gave a different meaning to
"the fields of France".

September 1, 1939

Where was I?
At home in our tranquil suburb?
In school, or was it too soon?
Playing with friends?
Reading in my room?
Still at the lake perhaps
or on a train
coming home.
I don't know what time of day it was,
don't think I even heard the news.
My parents surely knew
but they must have said
best not tell the children.
Nor did I know of Kristallnacht
Anschluss
the Sudetenland
Munich.

It was probably summery still,
the leaves unchanged,
a calm September day.

December 7, 1941

For the young the war was far away,
something happening in Europe,
something vague.
School was more real,
Freddie Appleton's house,
our meadow,
the orchard,
the pond.

Then that day
it invaded our home,
the voices on the radio
somber, hushed,
solemn, stentorian, outraged.
My father was on the phone
talking in urgent tones.
He was activated,
reporting for duty the next day,
and we would follow him,
exiled from Eden
through no sin of our own.

A Boy's War

I was seven
when it began,
Anschluss, then Munich—
Kristallnacht slipped by
wholly unnoticed by me—
and within a year
blitzkrieg was loosed on Europe.

Then Dunkirk and the fall of France.
I heard the news on the radio,
but it didn't seem so momentous.
It was part of life as I knew it,
along with boyhood fantasies
like the warplanes I drew
and learned to recognize
daydreaming of playing the hero one day
by spotting an enemy.

If it hadn't been for my parents' hushed tones
even Pearl Harbor might have seemed
like some extravagant sports event,
for in my boyish mind
death was unreal,
and war a game.

In Memory of

Another World War II pilot gone.
Obit on a back page of The Times
"Pilot who downed Yamamoto dies at 84."
A photo of three lean young men in khakis
looking as if they never could be 80
posed in front of a fighter plane
Pacific palms in the background.
He began high school about the time I was born
and I began it the year he downed the infamous
    admiral.
My cousin Bob was a fighter pilot in that war,
so much a part of my adolescent imagination,
and it's almost as if the young man in the photo,
now, unbelievably, deceased,
were my kin.

Obit the same day for Percy Goring, 106,
last British survivor of Gallipoli.
When I was a boy it was the last veteran of the Civil
    War
and, when a young man, the Spanish American.
For earlier generations it was the Revolutionary
the Hundred Years, the Punic, the Persian,
always one within reach of living memory,
and always some last veteran
to nurture
nostalgia for old wars.

The Veterans

Of all the young men
who went to war after '41
still believing
in everlasting love
and life too long to think about,
confident they would return,
though only some did,
and confident they would get ahead,
though only some did,
most have fallen
from the ranks.

Of those few who remain,
the hard muscles
that propelled them
across the fields of death,
and life,
have shrunk,
and their muscular ambitions
have withered.
Now they look back
and remember those days
when they went to war
fit and trim
and felt they could outrun mortality.

I Was a Soldier Once

I was a soldier once, and young
though I never fought in a war,
no buddy of mine died in one
and indeed I don't remember
that any Americans fought in those years
or even if there was a war at the time.
I was a peacetime soldier,
drafted,
with no dreams of glory,
though I came to dream of waging war
on the military mind.
Oh, there were intelligent ones
but they took care to hide their intelligence.
It was OK to be smart,
but thoughtful, no,
nor inclined to see things in shades of grey.
Decisive was the ticket—
though it didn't matter where that decisiveness
    led—
respectful of tradition and authority
and the primate hierarchies of rank.
So it was a time of disgruntled draftees
overeducated and disdainful
hating every minute of their military lives,
and I was one.
But I survived.

Citizen Soldier

I was a soldier once
in a faraway land
though not on death's hallowed ground.
It was during an undeclared peace
and I went to an office every day
where I battled armies of paper,
and by night toiled in other ways
in beer halls and brothels.

There were field exercises, to be sure,
and Saturday parades
where we practiced maneuvers
unseen in warfare
since the redcoats were ambushed by the
    minutemen,
and our company commander
polished his patent leather holster
lovingly as an apple,
while we waited to march by
sharply aligned
as if all of one mind
our bodies going one way
our minds another.

Vor der Kaserne

There comes a time in May
when the light of streetlamps
is filtered through leaves—
no more winter-naked glare—
when the nights are balmy
and the blood stirs,
when I think of the barracks in Verdun
where I was a soldier once,
of the chestnut trees of France
filtering the light
and of the graves of the Great War
surrounding the town,
and I think of a song from another war.

Aftermath

We were quartered in the *Heidelberg Kaserne*
a *Wermacht* billet not long before.
(Were those their beds we used
or did we bring our own?)

The town was in good condition,
spared the Baedeker raids,
thanks to the University, I suppose,
and had been sanctified since the war
by the *wirtschaftswunder,*
the economic miracle.
The natives were plump
and didn't treat us like conquerors
and we didn't play the role with them.

It was like a theme park
for young soldiers
where we could bask in the aura
of this emblematic place,
the streets of our imagination
peopled by ghostly duelists
with their trophy scars,
the actual streets
by camp followers
more hospitable even
than Disneyland hostesses;
an orderly scene
nothing like Dresden,
or after the Thirty Years War.
This storm passed over the town
preserving it as a playground
for our boys.

Roll Call

In my twenties
I was a conscript in Europe,
and once, on leave, visited London
where I stayed at The Soldiers', Seamen's &
    Airmen's Club
near Trafalgar station,
a location that might have been chosen for its
    name,
that of a battle, of course,
but also of a cape in southwestern Spain,
transposed to England like booty of war.

An old marine
sat in the lobby most of the day
smoking a meerschaum pipe.
He had enormous mustaches
and always wore his dress blues.

The plaque on my cubicle door read,
"To the Queen's own Eighteenth Hussars.
In honor of their valiant services.
Violet Lady Beaumont"
The one on the door next to mine
was dedicated to
"Lt. Harry Haversham
Died Bloemfontein, February 1900."

Remembering Vientiane

Known among early European visitors
for their gentleness and insouciance,
they lingered in a backwater
of this turbulent century.

I lived in their capital
near the broad Mekong
on a dirt lane
bracketed by old wooden temples,
unpainted and weather-stained,
with their muffled bells
and slow traffic of orange-robed monks.

Only roosters
disturbed the peace
until tanks came
clogging the narrow streets,
grinding them under ridged treads,
spewing manic metal
onto roofs and shutters,
like the rhetoric
of clashing ideologies.

And bodies erupted
from the river's smooth surface.

Lahore

There were massacres in Lahore
when the new nation was formed.
I learned this only recently
though I lived there once,
knew the city, even its side streets
where mosques
mingled with homes,
knew Akbar's palace, Jahangir's,
the gardens of Shah Jahan,
Zamzama, the massive cannon
on which Kipling's youthful hero perched
but the city never revealed its bloody past to me.
I saw no memorials,
no blood stains on the streets,
no ghosts—
even the ghosts erased—
and heard no mention of the killing.
The city was pure,
cleansed of Hindu and Sikh,
absolution complete.

Angkor

During centuries
temples spread
rich in sculpture
of the Buddha, deities, demons,
elephants, lions, kings,
fluent friezes depicting the Ramayana,
buildings as intricate as Rubik's cube,
towers like spiked flowers,
countless visages of Avalokiteshvara,
the compassionate one,
watching over the four corners of the world.

Then an empire fell
the temples were abandoned
and jungle returned.
Trees grew from colossal Buddha heads
gripping their cheeks
with gnarled fingers.
Massive roots
twisted and toppled
structures of heavy stone.

Later men came back
laboring the better part of a century
to free the sanctuaries,
felling the tall trees
severing the constricting roots
painstakingly fitting stone to stone,
until war too returned.

Martyrs: Afghanistan

Mourned in Iowa,
the Bronx,
upstate New York,
anywhere young men dream
of heroic deeds,
or see no better opportunity,
and thousands more dying,
collaterally.
For what?
To deprive our enemies of a base
of which they have many
and need few.

Boots on the Ground

Put boots on the ground, they said,
as if they were dragons' teeth
which, sown, sprout spectral armies
that fade away once battle is done,
leaving no blood behind.

They said nothing about
the men and boys
who would no longer have feet
to wear those boots,
or would wear them to their graves.

Forward to the Past

Fukuyama was wrong.
It wasn't the end of history
when the (most recent) evil empire collapsed.
History was merely pulling up
to go into reverse,
back to Coolidge, Harding, Hoover
when the corporate cocks ruled the roost
and the President was their hen,
back to when the bigger birds
got most of the corn,
weren't ashamed to flaunt their feathers
and convinced the barnyard with their crowing.
And war is rampant again,
though these days it may be a matter of mostly
Bush wars.

The Things They Carry

I hear casually booming voices in the street
and, looking out the window, see
two boys in their early teens.
From the sound they might be men,
and I think of such almost-men
some will grow up to be soldiers,
carry their childhood fantasies
into the world,
like flags,
and I think,
in another part of that world
these men-children would bear arms,
kill and be killed
before becoming men.
What could be more manly?

Where Have All the Young Men Gone?

Each someone's beloved
snuffed out
in the paddies of Nam
in the hills of Korea
on the beaches of Normandy,
swallowed by the greedy god
but leaving behind
those who remember
one who was
and always will be
young
embalmed in a long-ago moment
but living still
in the hearts of those
who loved him.

All the Brave Men

The soldier's glory
is the widow's, mother's, grief.
The shot that hits its mark
stops the heart
of a husband, father, brother, son.
The bomb that interdicts supplies
takes life from those who never wanted war.
The cannon is callous
in its choice of targets
disinterested as a beast of prey
in its choice of a meal.

Memorial

Reading the name
of a young man who died in war
saddens us.
Yet more the names of thousands
engraved in granite, or marble,
their parents' hopes and dreams
interred in stone.
All that remains are a few keepsakes,
and memories
of newborns, toddlers, vulnerable boys,
youths becoming men,
those now sad memories,
and names carved in cold stone.

Who wanted those wars?
Their leaders of course,
but all too often those same young men,
and all too often
those who mourn for them.

The Unnamed Dead

"Car Bomb Kills 7 in Baghdad"
reads the headline in *The Times*.
Just a number.
We see them every few days,
these numbers,
sometimes small enough to count on your fingers,
sometimes a good deal larger.
Nothing but numbers,
no names,
no history.
Our military casualties
are listed daily
under the heading "Names of the Dead"
with rank, unit, hometown.
But those civilians,
just not news,
hardly even people.

Numbers Don't Speak

Sectarian Attack Kills 15 in Nigeria
the headline said.
Lots of headlines.
Five or fifteen dead,
fifty, five hundred,
a hundred thousand.
Sixty thousand the government says.
One hundred and fifty thousand
say human rights activists.

Numbers, just numbers.
It's hard to care.
Numbers don't breathe,
or stop breathing.
Numbers don't have mothers or fathers
brothers, sisters, children, husbands, wives.
Numbers don't speak
or stop speaking.
Numbers don't tell their stories.
No stories are told of them.
They're just numbers
It's hard to care.

The Grenade

A handy thing the grenade.
An ergonomic weapon.
Fits nicely in a man's hand.
Neither too heavy nor too light.
Good for throwing.

Named after the pomegranate,
because of its shape,
but might as well be because of the seeds it
    contains,
sowing death or at least dismemberment.

It's an economical weapon too
disposing efficiently
of whole groups of enemy
rather than trying to make them dead one by one.
It's a disassembly line.

Grenades don't help us win, however,
for the enemy has them too.
The same might be said for most weapons.
They help us only as long as they're new,
which is seldom for long.
But we have to retain them even then
to meet the competition
lest we suffer insolvency
in the marketplace of death.

The Weapons Economy

Measured in weapons
human progress has been great.
Our weapons are more ingenious
effective
efficient
reliable
precise
deadly
user friendly
than ever before.

Our anti-personnel weapons
spew projectiles
as if they were ladling out beans.
Our bombs can fly through a door or window
without touching the frame.
They can pinpoint a man on a toilet seat
or the toilet seat under the man.
In the dark they home in on heat
like mosquitoes.
We can blow up cities in a flash
turning populations into toasted marshmallows.

Our gross national destructiveness has soared.

The Great and the Good

they say.
Why not the great and the bad,
for aren't more of them bad than good?
Think Napoleon,
Alexander,
who wasn't so bad, I suppose,
compared to some,
but all those conquests
and those who died for them,
for what purpose other than glory?
Or Caesar.
Or Charlemagne.
Frederick the Great.
Peter the you know who.
Aren't most of those we glorify conquerors?

"The great and the bad"
seems more apt.

To Those without Whom We Couldn't Win

The patriots, the hawks,
the pundits, the editorial writers,
the legislators, the advisors,
all those brave men who spur us on
and hold our coats and cheer.
Without them how could we ever win a war?

www.ingramcontent.com/pod-product-compliance
Lightning Source LLC
Chambersburg PA
CBHW061346040426
42444CB00011B/3115